MARVELS OF TECHNOLOGY

ENTERTAINMENT & INFO TECH

by
Anita Loughrey and Alex Woolf

Minneapolis, Minnesota

Credits

Cover and title page, © ImageFlow/Shutterstock and © Sandipkumar Patel/iStock 4MR, © Event Horizon/Shutterstock; 4BR, © Macrovector/Shutterstock; 4–5, © Renata Photography/Shutterstock; 6–7T, © FUN FUN PHOTO/Shutterstock; 6–7B, © Martin Sanders/Beehive Illustration; 7TL, © Public domain/Wikimedia commons; 7ML, © giocalde/Shutterstock; 7BR, © guruXOX/Shutterstock; 8TR, © QBR/Shutterstock; 8M, © CapturePB/Shutterstock; 8–9, © Triff/Shutterstock; 9BL, © Aljawad/Wikimedia commons; 10TR, © TimBurgess/Shutterstock; 10M, © Porawas Tha/Shutterstock; 10BL, © Smithsonian Institution/Wikimedia commons; 10–11, © Kjetil Kolbjornsrud/Shutterstock; 11BR, © Africa Studio/Shutterstock; 12MR, © Dja65/Shutterstock and Everett Collection/Shutterstock; 12BL, © IEEE/Wikimedia commons; 12–13, © Krivosheev Vitaly/Shutterstock and © AlexLMX/Shutterstock and © pixfly/Shutterstock; 14B, © violetblue/Shutterstock; 14–15, © Andrey_Popov/Shutterstock and © ViewStock/Getty Images; 15TL, © Juris Teivans/Shutterstock; 15BL, © Petr Malyshev/Shutterstock; 16ML, © Kaspars Grinvalds/Shutterstock; 16BL, © Ann Rodchua/Shutterstock; 16–17, © metamorworks/Shutterstock, 17, © Gorodenkoff/Shutterstock; 17BL, © FLHC MDB8/Alamy; 18ML, © 15Studio/Shutterstock; 18MR, © Audio und werbung/Shutterstock; 18BL, © Wellcome collection; 18–19, © Africa Studio/Shutterstock; 19B, © SHEILA TERRY/Science Photo Library; 20TR, © Golubovy/Shutterstock; 20B, © Pixel Enforcer/Shutterstock; 20–21, © Pelikh Alexey/Shutterstock; 21TR, © katacarix/Shutterstock; 21ML, © Triff/Shutterstock; 21BL, © US Library of Congress/Wikimedia commons; 22BL, © MIGUEL G. SAAVEDRA/Shutterstock; 22–23, © sint/Shutterstock; 23MR, © Mike Flippo/Shutterstock; 23BL, © Public domain/Wikimedia commons; 24B, © Wachiwit/Shutterstock; 24–25, © carballo/Shutterstock; 25TL, © Public domain/Wikimedia commons; 25ML, © PandaWild/Shutterstock; 26ML, © Colin Hui/Shutterstock; 26BL, © Gage Skidmore/Wikimedia commons; 26–27, © wavebreakmedia/Shutterstock; 27BL, © Bohbeh/Shutterstock; 28M, © Zern Liew/Shutterstock; 28BL, © Shutterstock; 28–29, © Dedi Grigoroiu/Shutterstock; 29BL, © Martin Sanders/Beehive Illustration; 30–31, © Toria/Shutterstock; 31TR, © flat_search1/Shutterstock; 31ML, © Rawpixel.com/Shutterstock; 31BL, © Paul Clarke/Wikimedia commons; 32ML, © DenPhotos/Shutterstock; 32–33, © Elegant Solution/Shutterstock; 33TL, © SA Torchi/Wikimedia commons; 34ML, © Elena Elisseeva/Shutterstock; 34MR, © dotshock/Shutterstock; 34BL, © US National Library of Medicine/Wikimedia commons; 34–35, © Rawpixel.com/Shutterstock and © fyv6561/Shutterstock and © MariaLev/Shutterstock; 36MR, © Akira Kaelyn/Shutterstock; 36ML, © Martin Sanders/Beehive Illustration; 36BL, © Timoni West; 36–37, © K_E_N/Shutterstock; 37TR, © RenysView/Shutterstock; 38ML, © ang intaravichian/Shutterstock; 38BL, © Theodore Scott/Shutterstock; 38–39, © Dmytro Zinkevych/Shutterstock; 39ML, © Martin Sanders/Beehive Illustration; 39BL, © dezign56/Shutterstock; 40TR, © successo images/Shutterstock; 40ML, © Shutterstock; 40BL, © Jaap Haartson; 40–41, © Stock Holm /Shutterstock; 41TR, © Monkey Business Images/Shutterstock; 41BR, © Denys Kurbatov/Shutterstock; 42ML, © Paolo Gallo/Shutterstock; 42M, © silvano audisio/Shutterstock; 42MR, © Margirita_Puma/Shutterstock; 42BR, © Friends Stock/Shutterstock; 42–43, © Fit Ztudio/Shutterstock; 43BL, © Frame Stock Footage/Shutterstock; 44BR, © carballo/Shutterstock; 45TL, © Akira Kaelyn/Shutterstock; 45BL, © Mike Flippo/Shutterstock; 47, © Dja65/Shutterstock and Everett Collection/Shutterstock

Bearport Publishing Company Product Development Team
President: Jen Jenson; Director of Product Development: Spencer Brinker; Managing Editor: Allison Juda; Associate Editor: Naomi Reich; Associate Editor: Tiana Tran; Art Director: Colin O'Dea; Designer: Kim Jones; Designer: Kayla Eggert; Product Development Assistant: Owen Hamlin

Statement on Usage of Generative Artificial Intelligence
Bearport Publishing remains committed to publishing high-quality nonfiction books. Therefore, we restrict the use of generative AI to ensure accuracy of all text and visual components pertaining to a book's subject. See BearportPublishing.com for details.

Library of Congress Cataloging-in-Publication Data is available at www.loc.gov or upon request from the publisher.

ISBN: 979-8-89232-085-6 (hardcover)
ISBN: 979-8-89232-617-9 (paperback)
ISBN: 979-8-89232-218-8 (ebook)

© 2025 Arcturus Holdings Limited
This edition is published by arrangement with Arcturus Publishing Limited.

North American adaptations © 2025 Bearport Publishing Company. All rights reserved. No part of this publication may be reproduced in whole or in part, stored in any retrieval system, or transmitted in any form or by any means, electronic, mechanical, photocopying, recording, or otherwise, without written permission from the publisher. Bearport Publishing is a division of Chrysalis Education Group.

For more information, write to Bearport Publishing, 5357 Penn Avenue South, Minneapolis, MN 55419.

Contents

Entertainment Tech. 4
Printing Presses. 6
Cameras. 8
Radios 10
TV. 12
3D Movies 14
Streaming Media 16
Remote Controls 18
Remote-Controlled Cars 20
Electric Guitars 22
Video Games 24
Home Computers 26
Smartphones and Tablets. 28
The Internet. 30
Wi-Fi. 32
Cloud Storage 34
Virtual Reality 36
Headphones 38
Wireless Speakers. 40
Entertainment for the Future 42

Review and Reflect 44
Glossary. 46
Read More 47
Learn More Online. 47
Index 48

Entertainment Tech

At its most basic, technology is simple. It's the application of scientific knowledge to create products that solve problems and make our lives more convenient, efficient, and fun. But what technology can do is pretty amazing.

Meeting Our Needs

New technologies are developed to meet our ever-evolving needs. For example, as our school, work, and home lives became more driven by electronic communication and online data, we needed more ways to access this info on the go. Laptops, tablets, smartphones, and smartwatches were all created to meet this need.

Solving Problems

Technology changes as our needs change. Most of the media we consume—music, TV shows, movies, photos, and news—gets transmitted digitally. This data can quickly fill a device's storage space and slow down its functionality. So, engineers developed cloud storage, a way to store our files and data on secure remote servers. This saves space on our devices and allows them to operate at superfast speeds.

Entertainment can now go almost anywhere you can!

Future Fun

Every day, designers are working to create exciting and innovative ways for us to interact and be entertained. We can watch the latest movies while camping in the wild, create playlists with millions of songs, download thousands of books, or escape our daily lives with virtual reality. Millions of digital experiences can all be contained within a single device the size of a deck of playing cards!

Printing Presses

Printing is old technology, but the way the printing press works has changed over time. Many printing presses use a process called offset lithography. First, the page to be printed is transferred photographically onto a thin metal plate. The image parts of the plate are coated with lacquer to attract ink, while the rest is covered with gum that attracts water. Then, the plate is curved around a cylinder and covered with water and ink. Only the lacquered parts of the plate pick up ink.

> Usually, only four colors of ink are used in printing: cyan, magenta, yellow, and black. Other colors can be created using these four inks.

Web Offset Lithography

The inked printing cylinder presses against a blanket cylinder. This soft rubber cylinder transfers the image onto paper. Since the printing plate doesn't directly touch the paper, this method is called offsetting. Many high-speed presses are web-fed. The paper comes into the press from a giant roll called a web.

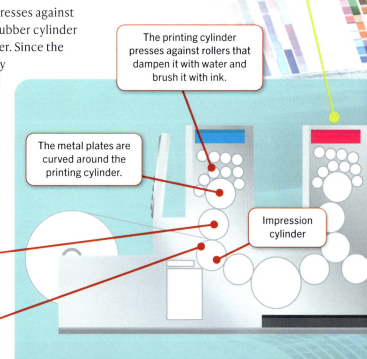

The printing cylinder presses against rollers that dampen it with water and brush it with ink.

The metal plates are curved around the printing cylinder.

Impression cylinder

The blanket cylinder transfers the image to the paper.

Paper feeds between the blanket and impression cylinders.

6

INVENTOR

Inventor: Johannes Gutenberg
Invention: Printing press
Date: 1450
The story: German blacksmith Johannes Gutenberg invented a form of movable type printing press on which individual letters could be moved around to form different words. A screw-type press stamped the inked metal letters onto the paper.

Computer-to-Plate

A lot of modern printing presses use desktop publishing software to determine where the text and images will go on each page. A digital image is transmitted directly from the computer to a printing plate, where it is coated with a light-sensitive chemical. Then, the image areas are burned onto the plate with lasers using ultraviolet light or heat.

The different inks have to be aligned correctly to produce the perfect print.

A web-fed printing press can produce more than 12 miles (19 km) of printed material in an hour.

Computer-to-plate technology produces higher quality printed material.

DID YOU KNOW? Printing was invented in China more than 1,000 years ago. Characters were carved onto wooden blocks that were dipped in ink and pressed onto parchment.

Cameras

If a person presses the button on a digital camera, the aperture, or hole at the front of the camera, briefly opens and closes. The opening lets light enter through the lens. An electronic light sensor captures the image and breaks it into millions of tiny pieces called pixels. A sensor measures the color and brightness of each pixel and stores it as a number.

The shutter lets light through to the sensor.

Shutter

The shutter is the mechanism that opens and closes the aperture. A slow shutter speed lets in more light, resulting in a brighter image, but objects in motion will appear blurry.

Shutter release button

Power switch

External flash shoe

Mode dial

This dial sets the camera to different preset shutter and exposure options. These camera modes may include landscape, portrait, and sport.

Image Editing

Image editing programs are used to adjust digital photos. To make an image 10 percent brighter, the programs increase the brightness number of each pixel by 10 percent.

DID YOU KNOW? During the Apollo 11 moon mission, astronauts left 12 cameras behind on the moon.

The menu button lets the user navigate the camera's setup options.

Information button

View finder

Zoom-in button

Automatic exposure and automatic focus lock

Zoom-out button

Delete button

Image playback button

The display screen lets the user see photos they have taken.

The selection pad lets the user scroll through the setting options and the pictures they took.

Inventor: Steven Sasson
Invention: Digital camera
Date: 1976
The story: American electrical engineer Steven Sasson designed a prototype digital camera. His bosses at Kodak were not impressed. The company thought no one would want to look at their pictures on a screen.

INVENTOR

9

Radios

Radio stations use antennae to send signals through the air carried by radio waves called carrier waves. This process is called modulation. There are two types of modulation: frequency modulation (FM) and amplitude modulation (AM). With FM radio, the number of carrier waves per second is altered. Meanwhile, in AM radio, a wave's size is changed.

Transmitter masts amplify outgoing signals from radio stations.

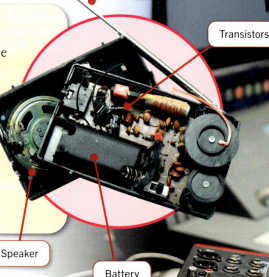

Antenna

Transistors

Transistor Radio

Radio signals are picked up by the antennae of individual radios. A radio's tuner allows the user to decide which radio wave frequency, or radio channel, to listen to. An amplifier is made up of one or more transistors, which boost the signal carried by the wave and send it to the speaker.

Speaker

Battery

INVENTOR

Inventor: Guglielmo Marconi
Invention: Radio
Date: 1895
The story: Italian inventor Guglielmo Marconi sent and received the first radio signals. His experiments stretched the distance that wireless communication could travel. In 1901, he successfully received a transmission in Canada from the United Kingdom. This helped establish a transatlantic radio service.

10   **DID YOU KNOW?** There are more than 40,000 radio stations around the world.

The microphone can be moved to different positions.

The microphone converts a radio DJ's voice into electrical signals that are then transmitted as radio waves.

Headphones let a DJ listen to other music to find new tracks while other songs are playing.

The mixing desk allows the DJ to smoothly fade different sounds in and out, such as songs, commercials, and in-studio programs.

Tuner

Tuner

A radio's antenna receives thousands of radio waves all the time. The tuner separates one wave from the rest by using a principle called resonance. The tuner resonates at and amplifies one particular frequency. The others are ignored.

TV

Many of today's high-definition, flat-screen televisions use LEDs, or light-emitting diodes. Their screens are made up of millions of tiny pixels that can be switched on or off to make a complete picture.

Behind every LED screen is a bright light. When an electric charge is applied to the liquid crystal inside each pixel, it changes its orientation by blocking or admitting the light.

Types of TVs

In LED televisions, each pixel is made up of three smaller red, green, and blue sub-pixels. The colored sub-pixels can be turned on and off very quickly by liquid crystals, which are like microscopic light switches, to make a colorful moving picture. OLED TVs are composed of a layer of organic molecules placed between two electrodes. They are thinner and lighter than LED televisions. The color contrast is also better, with darker blacks and brighter whites.

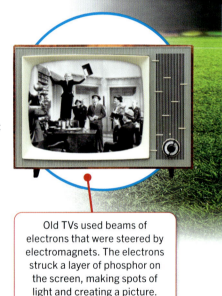

Old TVs used beams of electrons that were steered by electromagnets. The electrons struck a layer of phosphor on the screen, making spots of light and creating a picture.

INVENTOR

Inventor: George H. Heilmeier
Invention: Liquid-crystal displays
Date: 1968
The story: American engineer George H. Heilmeier discovered electro-optic effects in liquid crystals. He showed how they could be manipulated with an electric charge. This led to the development of the first liquid-crystal displays for calculators, watches, and TVs.

DID YOU KNOW? There are smart windows that use liquid-crystal display technology to switch from opaque to transparent at the push of a button.

Transmission

There are a few ways that radio waves can carry TV signals to individual TVs. They can be sent from powerful antennae or through underground cables. TV signals are also beamed as microwaves up to satellites in space and back to Earth. The TV turns the signals back into pictures.

3D Movies

Humans have stereoscopic vision. This means each eye sees a slightly different image. Both images are sent to the brain, where they are processed and combined into one. This gives us depth perception. Three-dimensional (3D) technology uses our stereoscopic vision to create 3D images by sending slightly different pictures to each eye.

Polarized Movies

Modern 3D movies use polarized light. Normal light is made up of waves that vibrate in multiple directions. Polarized light waves are filtered so they vibrate in only one direction. 3D movies are projected through different polarized filters, one sent to each eye.

Images sent to the right eye are polarized on the vertical plane.

Images sent to the left eye are polarized on the horizontal plane.

Each lens is filtered to let only one kind of polarized light through. That way, each eye sees a different version of the same frame. The brain combines them to create the 3D experience.

14

Active 3D TV

With active 3D TV, images for left and right eyes are displayed alternately. This requires shutter glasses powered by batteries with lenses coated with liquid crystal. Each lens quickly alternates between opaque and transparent, so each eye sees only the frame it's supposed to.

3D films are made using two camera lenses set side by side. Traditionally, the lenses had red and blue filters.

An infrared signal from a special emitter near the TV tells the shutter glasses when to change each lens.

INVENTION

Inventor: Kenneth J. Dunkley
Invention: 3-DVG glasses
Date: 1986
The story: While researching human vision, American physicist Kenneth J. Dunkley found that by blocking two points in someone's peripheral vision, he could transform two-dimensional images into 3D images. His 3-DVG glasses made ordinary photos look 3D.

DID YOU KNOW? Manufacturers are figuring out how to build lenses into TV screens. This would let viewers watch 3D movies without using glasses.

15

Streaming Media

Today, most people play music, listen to the radio, and watch TV shows and movies on devices that use the internet. In the early days of digital media, this content had to be downloaded onto a device's hard drive. This took up lots of storage space, slowing down a device's functions. With the advancement of streaming media, however, users can now experience content as it simply passes through their device and then goes away.

When the user selects a song to listen to or a movie to watch, that digital file is retrieved from a remote server on the World Wide Web. The file is broken down into smaller packets of data and sent in a continuous stream to the user's device. After the user is done, the streamed file is automatically deleted from the device.

A strong high-speed internet connection is important when playing streaming media. There is a lag time between the content being sent from the remote server and the content being received by the device. A slow or weak connection will lengthen this lag and sometimes create interruptions in the stream. This makes for a glitchy, discontinuous, and very frustrating listening or viewing experience.

DID YOU KNOW? The first streaming media may have started in 1881. A French company offered the chance to hear opera and theater performances over the telephone.

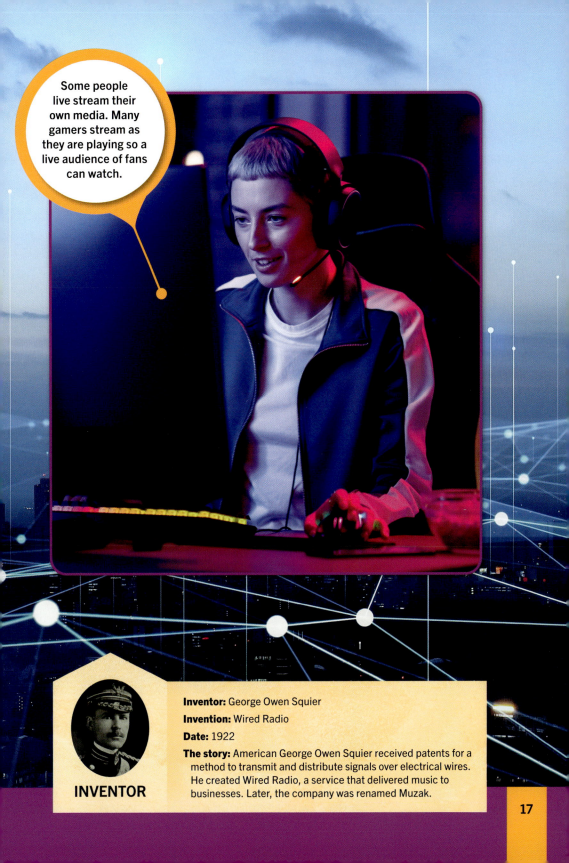

Some people live stream their own media. Many gamers stream as they are playing so a live audience of fans can watch.

INVENTOR

Inventor: George Owen Squier
Invention: Wired Radio
Date: 1922
The story: American George Owen Squier received patents for a method to transmit and distribute signals over electrical wires. He created Wired Radio, a service that delivered music to businesses. Later, the company was renamed Muzak.

Remote Controls

The first wireless remote controls used ultrasound, a high-pitched sound, to change the channel and volume on TVs. When a user pushed a button on the control, it clicked and struck a bar inside. Each bar produced a sound at a particular frequency that was identified by a receiver in the television. However, there were problems with using ultrasound in remotes. Dogs and some humans could hear the piercing signals, and readers were sometimes triggered by other noises.

Infrared Remotes

Infrared remotes use an LED to transmit signals. Pulses of invisible infrared light carry signals from a remote to the electrical device. The device needs to be in the line of sight for the LED to work. Infrared remotes have a range of about 30 feet (9 m). The signal carries binary code to represent commands, such as power on and volume down.

Using a smartphone, a user can control electrical devices in their smart home from anywhere in the world.

Radio Frequency Remotes

Radio frequency remotes have a greater range than infrared remotes. They can work at distances of about 100 ft. (30 m) or more. They are useful for opening and closing garages, locking and unlocking cars, and setting car alarms. They transmit at frequencies intended to reduce interference from other radio waves.

INVENTOR

Inventor: Nikola Tesla
Invention: Remote-controlled boat
Date: 1898
The story: Serbian-American inventor Nikola Tesla used radio waves to control the motor in a small boat. He unveiled his remote-controlled boat as part of the Electricity Exhibition of 1898 at Madison Square Garden. The crowd thought it was quite magical because very little was known about radio waves in those days.

18

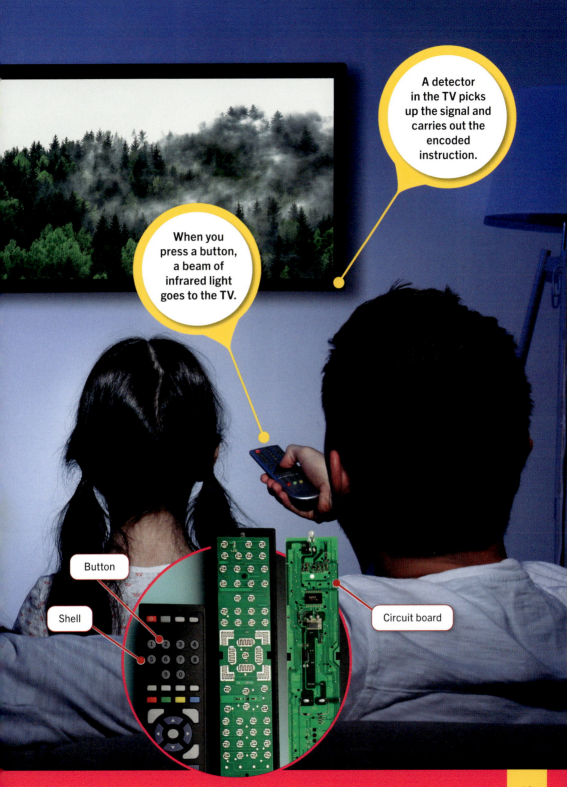

DID YOU KNOW? The *New Horizons* space probe uses remote-control technology to explore beyond our solar system.

19

Remote-Controlled Cars

A remote-controlled car can be moved from a distance using a radio transmitter. The transmitter sends a command signal carried by radio waves to a receiver in the car. This signal activates motors inside the car, making it start or stop, or causing its wheels to turn. The car can be powered by batteries or fuel.

The transmitter has its own power source, usually a battery, and sends signals on a frequency that the car is tuned to receive.

A circuit board is used for receiving commands.

The circuit board sends commands to specific parts of the car.

The antenna receives the signal and sends it to the circuit board.

The motor turns the wheels and steers the car.

A battery powers most remote-controlled cars

DID YOU KNOW? The first radio-controlled car was a miniature Ferrari. It went on sale in 1966.

Engine and Fuel

In a fuel-driven, remote-controlled car, the fuel is a mixture of nitromethane and methanol. A blend of castor oil and synthetic oil is added to the fuel to provide lubrication and cooling. The engine works the same way as in a regular-sized car.

The battery and the circuit board are inside the shell of the car, along with the engine and fuel tank.

In 1997, NASA's *Sojourner* rover became the first radio-controlled vehicle to drive on Mars.

INVENTOR

Inventor: John Hays Hammond Jr.
Invention: Radio-guided torpedo
Date: 1914
The story: The American John Hays Hammond Jr. is called the father of radio control. He invented a target-seeking system, which enabled a remote-controlled torpedo to locate an enemy ship's searchlights.

Electric Guitars

When an electric guitar string is plucked, the vibration is detected by a magnet called a pickup. The pickup is wound with a coil of very fine wire. It converts the vibration into an electric signal, which passes through a circuit that adjusts the signal's tone and volume. This electric signal then flows through an amplifier to a speaker, which turns it into sound.

Pickups

Pickups are electromagnets mounted under a guitar's strings. Electromagnets are a type of magnet that converts motion into electric energy. Vibrations in the strings produce a corresponding vibration in the pickup's magnetic field, creating an electrical signal.

Headstock and Neck

The headstock contains the pegs used for tuning. The neck contains the fingerboard and frets to help the player know where their fingers should be placed to make a note.

Body | Bridge | Pickup

A guitar is tuned by turning the pegs, which tightens and loosens the strings.

The volume and tone controls adjust the frequency of the electric signal to produce different sounds.

22

Video Games

To make a video game, computer programmers must first write the software. Programmers write millions of lines of code, or computer language instructions, to create a game's storylines and characters. The code must allow for all possible choices that players can make in the game. Once the coding is complete, the game is tested to fix any software errors before it is released to the public.

Game Consoles

A console is a highly specialized computer. It has an operating system to organize and control a game's hardware and software. The console also has random-access memory to store information as a game is played, providing the necessary speed for an interactive experience.

Headphones with built-in microphones let players talk to one another from anywhere in the world.

Portable Consoles

Today's portable game consoles feature more immersive player experiences. They contain devices to track the player's movements and gestures. An accelerometer measures a console's acceleration, and a gyroscope measures its tilting motion. Some consoles also contain a haptic feedback system to give the player the sense of touching objects in the game.

INVENTION

Inventor: Ralph Baer
Invention: First game console
Date: 1969
The story: German-born American inventor Ralph Baer created the Brown Box. It was a prototype for the first multiplayer, multiprogram video game system.

The first video game was called Pong. It was a virtual game of table tennis, with two lines for rackets and a moving dot for the ball. Players had to stop the ball from going past their racket.

A controller is needed to play most video games.

DID YOU KNOW? In the original arcade version of Donkey Kong, Mario was called Jumpman. The character was a carpenter, not a plumber.

25

Home Computers

A computer is essentially an information processor. First, it receives data as inputs from a keyboard, mouse, or scanner. The data goes through a central processing unit according to programmed instructions. Finally, it outputs the data via a monitor, printer, or speaker.

Central Processing Unit

A computer's brain is called the central processing unit, or CPU. It is a chip containing millions of transistors. Each transistor is like an individual brain cell. The central processing unit executes stored instructions and performs calculations.

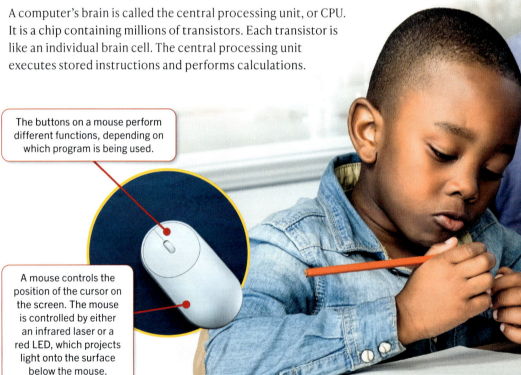

The buttons on a mouse perform different functions, depending on which program is being used.

A mouse controls the position of the cursor on the screen. The mouse is controlled by either an infrared laser or a red LED, which projects light onto the surface below the mouse.

INVENTOR

Inventor: Steve Wozniak
Invention: Apple I
Date: 1976
The story: American inventor Steve Wozniak co-founded the computer company Apple. He designed and made the first affordable home computer. It had a typewriter-like keyboard connected to a TV and was called the Apple I.

Monitor

The keyboard lets the user input data.

Hard drive

Built-in speakers

Mouse

Scanner

Printer

Memory

Computers have two kinds of memory. Random-access memory, or RAM, stores and retrieves data and software programs. When the computer is switched off, the RAM is deleted. Read-only memory, also called ROM, is where data is stored when the computer is off. Memory is measured in bytes.

Memory	Size
Bit	Single binary digit (1 or 0)
Byte	8 bits
Kilobyte (KB)	1,024 bytes
Megabyte (MB)	1,024 kilobytes
Gigabyte (GB)	1,024 megabytes
Terabyte (TB)	1,024 gigabytes
Petabyte (PB)	1,024 terabytes
Exabyte (EB)	1,024 petabytes

DID YOU KNOW? The first hard drive was made in 1979. It held only 5 MB of data.

27

Smartphones and Tablets

Smartphones and tablets are basically mobile computers. They have operating systems that run individual software programs called applications, or apps. There are apps for everything from communicating with friends to streaming TV shows and forecasting the weather.

The photo app contains all the user's photographs, videos, and screenshots.

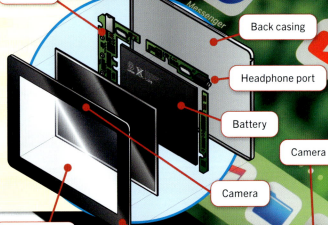

Speaker

Back casing

Headphone port

Battery

Camera

Camera

Front casing

Touchscreen

Touchscreen

The screen of a smartphone or tablet has a transparent layer of material that stores an electrical charge. When a user touches it, sensors detect a change in the electric current. Then, the software commands an action to be performed.

INVENTION

Inventor: Martin Cooper
Invention: Handheld portable phone
Date: 1973
The story: American telecommunications developer Martin Cooper helped produce the first handheld portable phone. The prototype was named DynaTAC. It was about the size and weight of a brick.

28 **DID YOU KNOW?** In 1926, Nikola Tesla predicted that we would one day have smartphones.

Alarms and timers can be set with the clock app.

Calendar

Settings

Text messages

A user's favorite songs can be stored and played back with the music app.

Phone contacts

Search engine

How mobile networks work

Base station

Caller

Base station

Mobile switching center

Receiver

Connectivity

Cell phones transmit and receive signals using radio waves. When a user begins a call, their phone sends radio waves to the nearest cell tower. This tower, or base station, then passes the signal along through a network of towers and switching centers to a base station near the receiver, which finally initiates the call on their end.

29

The Internet

The word *internet* is short for interconnected network. It is a global network of computers that enables communication, data transfer, and information sharing. Computers, cell phones, and other devices can connect through various kinds of hardware—including routers, servers, mobile phone towers, and satellites—which are linked by cables or radio signals. For the internet to work, it also needs protocols, or sets of rules that enable devices to understand one another.

World Wide Web

The World Wide Web is a network of websites that use the internet. It uses two protocols: hypertext transfer protocol (HTTP) and hypertext markup language (HTML). HTTP enables devices to communicate and swap files over the internet. HTML allows devices to understand the files they receive and display them correctly.

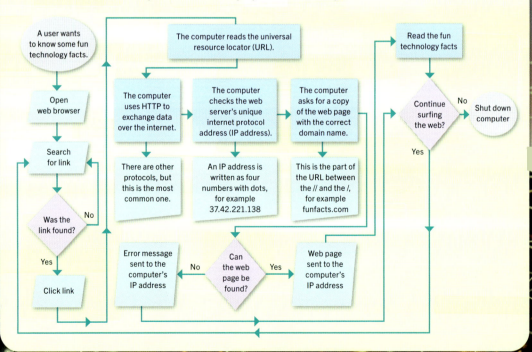

DID YOU KNOW? In 1971, American programmer Ray Tomlinson sent the first email.

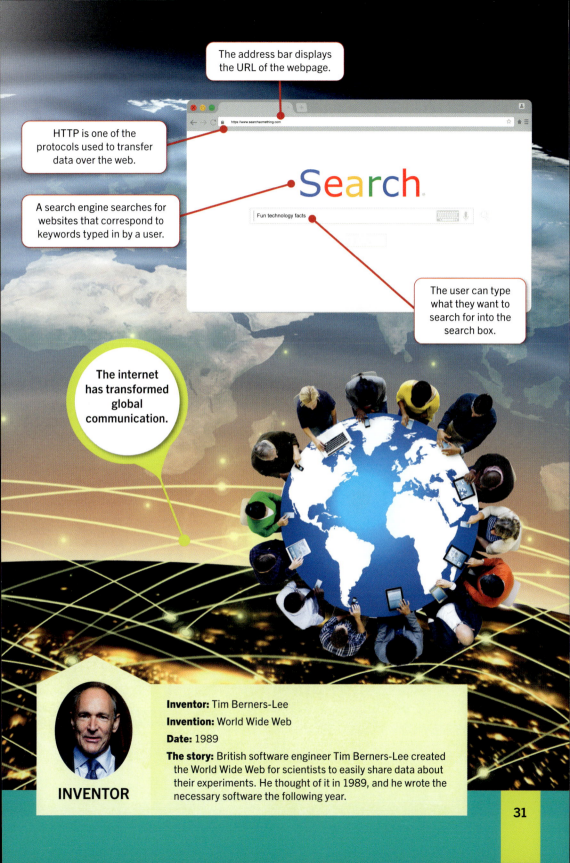

The address bar displays the URL of the webpage.

HTTP is one of the protocols used to transfer data over the web.

A search engine searches for websites that correspond to keywords typed in by a user.

The user can type what they want to search for into the search box.

The internet has transformed global communication.

INVENTOR

Inventor: Tim Berners-Lee
Invention: World Wide Web
Date: 1989
The story: British software engineer Tim Berners-Lee created the World Wide Web for scientists to easily share data about their experiments. He thought of it in 1989, and he wrote the necessary software the following year.

31

Wi-Fi

Wi-Fi is a technology that uses radio waves to transmit information wirelessly across a network. A computer's wireless adapter converts data into a radio signal, which it transmits to a router with an antenna. The router converts it back into data to be sent to the internet through an Ethernet cable. The system also works in reverse. Multiple devices can link to the same Wi-Fi network through a single router.

Some fire and smoke alarms have Wi-Fi connections.

Footage from security cameras can be viewed using Wi-Fi.

Heating and cooling can be set from a Wi-Fi enabled device.

Wi-Fi connected devices can be controlled using an app on a smartphone or tablet.

DID YOU KNOW? Many people assume the term Wi-Fi is short for something, but it doesn't actually stand for anything.

INVENTOR

Inventor: John O'Sullivan
Invention: Wireless connectivity
Date: 1990
The story: Australian electrical engineer John O'Sullivan and his team created microchips for wireless connection. The microchips increased signal transmission speeds by splitting the signals into smaller components and then recombining them at the receiver.

Wireless Local Area Network

A Wireless Local Area Network is a Wi-Fi network that can be used in a limited area, such as a home, school, or office building. Users can move around within the network and still be connected.

- Lights can be turned on and off or have the brightness changed using Wi-Fi.

- A garage door can be opened and closed at the push of a button without the driver having to leave the car.

- The timer on an oven or stove can be set and controlled.

- The preferred settings of water temperature can be easily saved.

Cloud Storage

Cloud storage is a method of saving data to vast, remote networks of powerful computers known as the cloud. This information can then be accessed via the internet. It is often a safe, convenient, and flexible way of storing data, compared with storing it on a computer or removable external drive.

Virtualization

Data is stored on large computers called servers. To store such large quantities of data, they use a technique called virtualization. Servers are subdivided into several smaller virtual machines, each of which runs on its own operating system. Virtualization reduces the number of actual physical machines needed.

Encryption

Data in the cloud is converted into a code through a process called encryption. To transmit data, every computer uses two sets of code known as encryption keys. A public encryption key is given to any computer that wants to send a file. A private key is unique to each computer. The two keys work together to keep data secure.

Information placed in the cloud is stored in large database servers.

For security, cloud providers keep their computers in multiple locations.

INVENTOR

Inventor: J. C. R. Licklider
Invention: The cloud
Date: 1962
The story: In the early 1960s, American computer scientist J. C. R. Licklider was one of the first to suggest the creation of a global network of computers. His ideas led to the development of the internet and cloud storage.

DID YOU KNOW? A user can edit documents in cloud storage by using different apps.

35

Virtual Reality

Virtual reality (VR) is a 3D, computer-generated environment. People can explore and interact with the environment by using a headset or by wearing clothing fitted with sensors. To create an immersive experience, a VR system needs to give users a minimum of a 100-degree field of view. It also needs a video speed of around 60 frames per second for the virtual world to be convincing.

Eye and Head Tracking

A VR system tracks the movements of a user's eyes and head using an accelerometer, a gyroscope, and a magnetometer. A computer analyzes data about the movement and adjusts the picture as the user looks around.

Sensors in the headset track a wearer's eye movements, causing the picture to shift when they look up, down, and to the side.

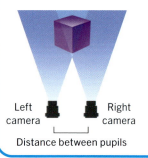

How to create 3D images for VR

Left projection
Right projection
Left eye
Right eye
Left camera
Right camera
Distance between pupils

Each lens angles its images to mimic how each eye sees things slightly differently, creating a 3D effect.

INVENTOR

Inventor: Timoni West
Invention: VR development
Date: 2018
The story: VR designer Timoni West is working on a project to enable developers to build games inside VR itself. She uses Unity, a 3D game engine that lets developers code and design in one environment.

36

VR Glove

A special VR glove lets the wearer feel as through they are touching virtual objects. The glove has internal pieces that tense and relax to simulate an experience of touch.

Eyewear lets the wearer manipulate virtual objects and perform actions in a virtual world.

DID YOU KNOW? In 2015, Marriot hotels used virtual reality to allow customers to explore hotels they might like to visit.

Headphones

Headphones deliver sounds straight to a user's ears. Electrical audio signals are sent to electromagnets, called coils, inside the headphones. These turn the signals into motion, causing thin, flexible cones known as diaphragms to vibrate. The vibrations then create the sound waves that the user hears. Different sounds can be delivered to each ear to produce a stereo effect.

Some earbuds must be plugged into a device's audio jack to listen to sounds.

Earbuds

Earbuds work like headphones, but all the elements are much smaller. The coil is at the back of the earbud. The diaphragm is near the front, often behind a layer of foam to protect the ears. Some earbuds are dome shaped to help amplify the sound.

INVENTION

Inventor: Nathaniel Baldwin
Invention: Headphones
Date: 1910
The story: American Nathaniel Baldwin is often credited as the inventor of modern headphones. He sent the prototype for his design to the U.S. Navy. They were impressed and wanted more. However, he could accept orders of only 10 at a time because he made them in his kitchen.

DID YOU KNOW? You should not play your music too loudly through headphones. It can damage your hearing.

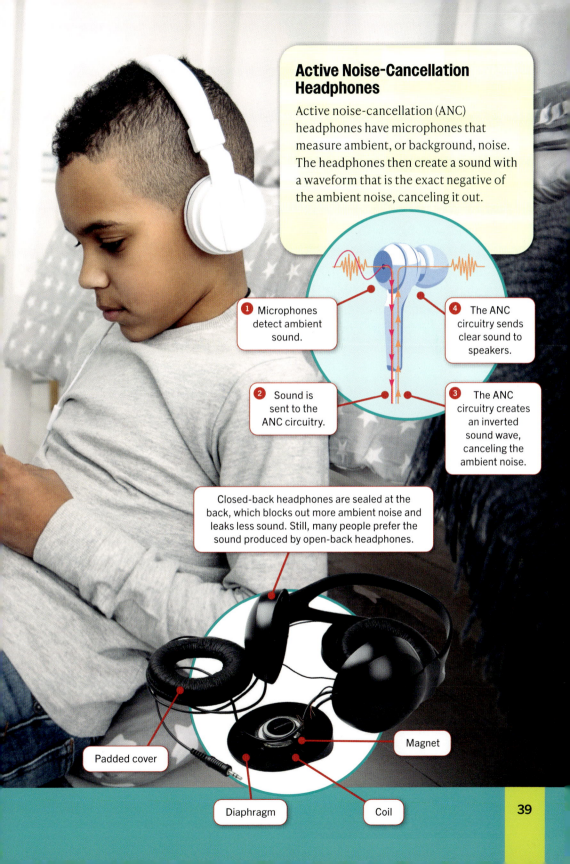

Active Noise-Cancellation Headphones

Active noise-cancellation (ANC) headphones have microphones that measure ambient, or background, noise. The headphones then create a sound with a waveform that is the exact negative of the ambient noise, canceling it out.

1. Microphones detect ambient sound.
2. Sound is sent to the ANC circuitry.
3. The ANC circuitry creates an inverted sound wave, canceling the ambient noise.
4. The ANC circuitry sends clear sound to speakers.

Closed-back headphones are sealed at the back, which blocks out more ambient noise and leaks less sound. Still, many people prefer the sound produced by open-back headphones.

Padded cover

Diaphragm

Coil

Magnet

39

Wireless Speakers

Bluetooth® speakers are wireless. They work by receiving radio signals from a smartphone or tablet. An antenna on the speakers detects the signals, and a receiver converts them into electric signals. A voice coil turns the signals into sound vibrations. Once connected with a paired device, the speakers can play sound initiated by that device.

Bluetooth can be used for one-to-one device communication or for sharing data between multiple devices.

Radio Waves

Bluetooth equipment transmits data via short-range radio waves. These waves can connect to a wide variety of electronic devices. Since Bluetooth uses radio waves, devices do not have to be in line of sight of each other.

INVENTOR

Inventor: Jaap Haartsen
Invention: Bluetooth
Date: 1994
The story: Dutch electrical engineer Jaap Haartsen was working in Sweden when he was asked to design a way for smartphones to share data wirelessly. He described his idea as "a walkie-talkie done on a world-scale."

Files can be shared between devices using Bluetooth technology.

Wireless Headset

A headset acts as both the transmitter and receiver of wireless signals. This lets people adjust sounds using the headset or their phone.

Most Bluetooth headsets have a built-in speaker and microphone.

DID YOU KNOW? Bluetooth was named after the Danish King Harald Bluetooth, who united Scandinavia during the 10th century.

41

Entertainment for the Future

Technology is always evolving. We went from carving images and words into stone, to printing text, and on to digitally displaying books on e-readers in a relatively short time. What's the next step forward? Only time will tell.

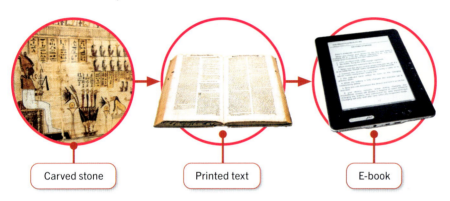

Carved stone | Printed text | E-book

The future of media may be faster, more personalized, more interactive, and more immersive. Soon, viewers may be able to choose a story, change the plot, and control the characters they see. The lines separating creator, creation, and consumer may blur and break down. It's a thrilling new era of digital entertainment!

VR devices may help healthcare providers care for patients from anywhere around the world.

What kinds of new and exciting games, apps, platforms, experiences, and devices can you dream up? With studying, hard work, and trial and error, maybe you will make that dream a reality!

43

Review and Reflect

Now that you've read about technology used in entertainment and information, let's review what you've learned. Use the following questions to reflect on your newfound knowledge and integrate it with what you already knew.

Check for Understanding

1. List two things that happen inside a printing press. *(See pp. 6-7)*

2. Name three parts of a camera and explain what each one does. *(See pp. 8-9)*

3. How do radio signals work? *(See pp. 10-11)*

4. How are LED and OLED TVs alike and different? *(See pp. 12-13)*

5. How do 3D movies work? *(See pp. 14-15)*

6. Why do we need high-speed internet to stream media? *(See pp. 16-17)*

7. What are the three kinds of remote controls? How are they different from one another? *(See pp. 18-19)*

8. What is the role of a magnet in an electric guitar? *(See pp. 22-23)*

9. Name three parts of a computer and describe what each one does. *(See pp. 26-27)*

10. What do sensors do in a smartphone or tablet? *(See pp. 28-29)*

11. What are two internet protocols? What do they do? *(See pp. 30-31)*

12. How does Wi-Fi work? *(See pp. 32-33)*

13. Name two parts of a VR system and describe what each one does. *(See pp. 36-37)*

14. How do headphones deliver sound? *(See pp. 38-39)*

15. What might someone use Bluetooth to do? *(See pp. 40-41)*

Making Connections

1. Name three things that can be controlled remotely.

2. Name at least three pieces of technology mentioned in this book that use radio waves.

3. Choose two inventors mentioned in the book. In your own words, describe what they made. How did their inventions affect society?

4. List two types of technology discussed in this book that can work together. How does one support the other?

In Your Own Words

1. Which type of technology described in this book is most useful or fun for you? What do you like about it?

2. Choose one tool or device mentioned in this book. What might be a potential improvement on its current capabilities?

3. Do you see any potential drawbacks or ethical concerns about any of the technology mentioned in this book? What might they be?

4. How do you think the technology used for entertainment and information will change in the future?

5. How do you think young people's lives were different from yours in the days before mobile computers and the internet?

Glossary

amplifier a device for increasing the amplitude of electrical signals, especially in sound reproduction

antenna a rod, dish, or other structure by which radio signals are transmitted or received

central processing unit the part of a computer in which operations are controlled and executed

circuit a path along which an electrical current can flow

electrode a conductor through which electricity enters or leaves an object

electron a particle within an atom that carries a negative electrical charge

frequency the number of times a wave completes a cycle in a second

hard drive a device that permanently stores and retrieves data on a computer

infrared having a wavelength greater than that of the red end of the visible light spectrum but less than that of microwaves

laser a device that generates an intense beam of light through the emission of photons from excited atoms or molecules

magnetic field a region around a magnet within which the force of magnetism acts

microwaves energy in the form of waves that are shorter than those of radio waves but longer than that of infrared radiation

operating system software that supports a computer's basic functions

router a device that forwards units of data to different parts of a computer network

sensor a device that detects, measures, or records an external event

server a computer program or device that provides services, such as data storage or sharing, to other devices

software the programs and operating systems used by a computer

telecommunication communication over a distance by, for example, wire or radio signals

transistor a tiny device that can amplify or switch an electronic signal

ultrasound sound waves with a frequency above the upper limit of human hearing

ultraviolet having a wavelength shorter than that of the violet end of visible light but longer than that of X-rays

Read More

Currie-McGhee, L. K. *Hi-Tech Jobs in Gaming (Exploring Hi-Tech Jobs).* San Diego: ReferencePoint Press, Inc., 2024.

Ignotofsky, Rachel. *The History of the Computer: People, Inventions, and Technology That Changed Our World.* Berkeley, CA: Ten Speed Press, 2022.

Kenney, Mary. *Gamer Girls: 25 Women Who Built the Video Game Industry.* Philadelphia: Running Press Teens, 2022.

MacCarald, Clara. *All about Virtual Reality (Cutting-Edge Technology).* Lake Elmo, MN: Focus Readers, 2023.

Learn More Online

1. Go to **www.factsurfer.com** or scan the QR code below.
2. Enter "**Entertainment Info Tech**" into the search box.
3. Click on the cover of this book to see a list of websites.

47

Index

accelerometers 36
amplifiers 10, 22–23
antennae 10, 13
batteries 15–21
binary code 18
cables 13, 30, 32
cameras 8–9, 15, 32
central processing unit 26
circuits 20–22
coding 24
coils 22, 38, 40
computers 4, 7, 24, 26–28, 30–32, 34, 36
cylinders 6
diaphragms 38
electric signals 22, 38, 40
electrodes 12
electromagnets 12, 22, 38
engines 21, 29, 31, 36
filters 14–15
frequency 10–11, 18, 20–22
fuel 20–21
gyroscopes 24, 36
infrared 15, 18–19, 26
internet 3, 30
laser 26
lenses 15
LEDs 12, 18, 26
liquid crystals 12, 15
magnet 22
magnetometers 36
microchips 33

microphones 11, 24, 39, 41
microwaves 13
motors 18, 20
operating systems 24, 28, 34
pixels 8, 12
polarized light 14
printing 6–7
radio waves 10–11, 13, 18, 20, 32, 40
random-access memory 24, 27
read-only memory 27
receivers 17–18, 20, 33, 40–41
remote control 18
routers 30–32
satellites 13, 30
sensors 8, 28, 36
servers 4, 16, 30–35
smartphones 4, 18, 28–29, 32, 40
software 7, 24, 27–28, 31
speakers 10, 22, 26–27, 39–41
switches 8, 12
tablets 4, 28
television 3–4, 12–13, 15–16, 18–19, 26, 28
tuners 10–11
ultrasound 18
vibrations 22, 38, 40
Wi-Fi 3, 29, 32–33

48